The Meditating Merma

Shevon Mullineaux

CW00417830

Illustrated by Jae Murphy

This story is dedicated to my children, Tate and Delilah.

Tate, to show that when you slow and focus, you make the BEST team player!

Delilah, always believe, always be curious and forever be you.

May your imagination be forever inspired

Copyright © 2023 Shevon Mullineaux

All rights reserved.

ISBN:9-7983-7237-656-4

This Book belongs to.

_____

_____

_____

The Meditating Mermaid.

Once upon a time, in the beautiful and peaceful ocean, there lived a young mermaid named Lilah.

Lilah was a curious and playful mermaid, who loved to explore the ocean, meet new sea creatures, and discover new things.

One day, Lilah was swimming near the Coral Reefs when she noticed a group of fish meditating. They were very still, with their eyes closed, and their breathing was slow and steady.
I've never seen fish so still, Lilah thought.

"Keep it up guys, you're doing excellent!"

"We are practicing meditation" Miss Lovely said. "It helps us to calm our minds and relax our bodies, would you like to join in?"
Lilah nodded eagerly and joined the fish.

She sat with her back straight, closed her eyes and took a big deep breath.

As she focused on her breathing, Lilah felt her mind and body becoming more and more relaxed. She felt a sense of peace and happiness that she had never experienced before and the whole world around her slipped away.

After the meditation, Lilah asked the fish to teach her more about meditation. They were so happy she had asked! They shared with her some basic techniques, such as counting her breaths, repeating a mantra, and visualising a peaceful place.

The mermaid spent the whole day learning with the fish.

Lilah went home and practiced all of these new techniques, every single day. She soon became a master at meditation. She was so thankful to have met those lovely fish on that beautiful day.

One day, while Lilah was meditating on the ocean floor, she heard a loud noise. She opened her eyes, and saw a huge ship sailing above her, dropping rubbish and pollution into the ocean.

"oh no..."

Lilah felt so sad and angry, but then she remembered her meditation skills. The mermaid took a huge deep breath, everything she had learned from the fish came flooding back to her.

Lilah counted her breaths, and repeated her mantra.

I am a calm yet strong mermaid and .... I am proud to call the ocean my home

She focused on the peaceful place she had visualised and let go of her emotions.
Lilah felt calm and focused, and was able to come up with a plan to save the ocean from pollution!

With the help of her friends, and lots of other sea creatures of the ocean, Lilah was able to stop the ship, and clean up the ocean.

But she couldn't have done it alone!

Lilah learned that meditation not only helped her to relax and find inner peace, but also gave her clarity and the strength to face challenges and make the world a better place. If you make a good team player, you can do anything!

THE END

Here are some meditation techniques for you to try:

Deep Breathing

Take slow deep breaths in through your nose (inhale) filling your belly with air. Then slowly breathe out (exhale) through your mouth.

Body Scan

Focus on each part of your body, starting with your toes and working all the way up to your head, take deep breaths and try to relax that part of your body.

Mantra Repetition

Repeat a simple word or phrase, such as 'peace', or 'I am calm', over and over again in your mind. This will help you to learn to focus and calm your mind.

Guided Imagery

Use the power of your imagination to create a peaceful scene in your mind. Describe, see, and experience your peaceful place, just like Lilah!

Dear Reader,

Thank you for joining us on our adventure through the ocean with Lilah, the meditating mermaid!

We hope you had as much fun reading it as we did writing it! We are so grateful that you took the time to explore with us.

We hope you will come back and visit us again soon, for more exciting adventures! Until then, keep reading and let your imagination soar!

Remember, focus on your breathing and visualise your peaceful place. Whenever you take your deep breaths, your mind will be transported to your favourite, calm spot.

Notes

Try writing your own mantra.

Well Done

Other books.

Graffiti colouring book 2023

Printed in Great Britain
by Amazon

16358030R00016